ADVENTURES OF CARMELO
Going to the Hospital

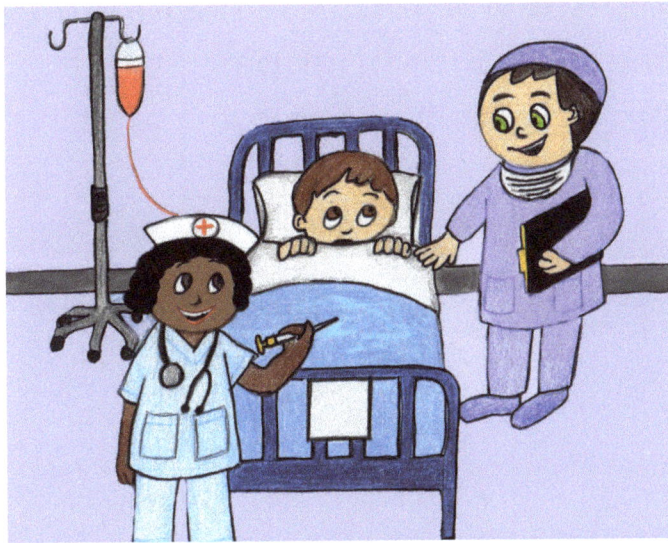

by fred berri

illustrated by ellen gillette

Adventures of Carmelo - Going to the Hospital
Copyright © 2020 frederic dalberri
ISBN: 978-1-7355131-3-3

Formatting by Janet Sierzant - La Maison Publishing, Inc.

The Adventures of Carmelo™
Other books in the series

Swim Survival Lesson
The Dentist
The Eye Doctor

DEDICATION

To Carmelo --
Ci vediamo quando ci vediamo.
See you when we see each other.
Love, Poppy

"Mommy, Mommy, my ear hurts.
My throat hurts again!"
I said, crying out.

"Oh, Carmelo," Mommy said.
"You've been getting
these sore throats and earaches often.
I'm going to call
Dr. Jessica so she can tell us why."

Soon, I had an appointment with Dr. Jessica.

"Hi, Carmelo," she said.
"Your Mommy tells me you're not feeling well.
Why don't you show me where it hurts?"

I pointed to my ear and my throat.
"They both hurt and it's hard to swallow,"
I told Dr. Jessica.

She looked in my ear with what doctors call an otoscope.
That's a big word, let's spell and sound it out...

O-T-O-S-C-O-P-E

Very good!

It has a light and a magnifying glass
so Dr. Jessica could see way into my ears.

"Well, I see from your chart, you've had many earaches and many sore throats," Dr. Jessica said. "And, you've had medicine to help you. Now, I want you to see a very special doctor."

"My friend Dr. Michele is a doctor just for your ears, nose and throat. She is called an E-N-T doctor. E is for your ears. N is for your nose. And the T is for your throat," she said.

Mommy made an appointment for me to see the special E-N-T doctor.

We had to wait many days.

Finally the day was here.
Off we went to see the special doctor, Dr. Michele.
She asked us lots of questions.

Do you remember what those letters mean?
E is for Ears. N is for Nose. T is for Throat.

When she explained more about what an E-N-T does, she pinched my nose and made me laugh.

She also examined me, looking in my ears and my throat.

Dr. Michele said. "Well, Carmelo,
it's time we did something about all these
earaches and sore throats you've been getting.
You're getting to be a big boy now.
You are four years old. I'm going to help you."

I was happy that I would not get earaches
and sore throats, but I was not happy
with what she said next.

"We will do surgery, Carmelo.
That will help you."

Surgery!

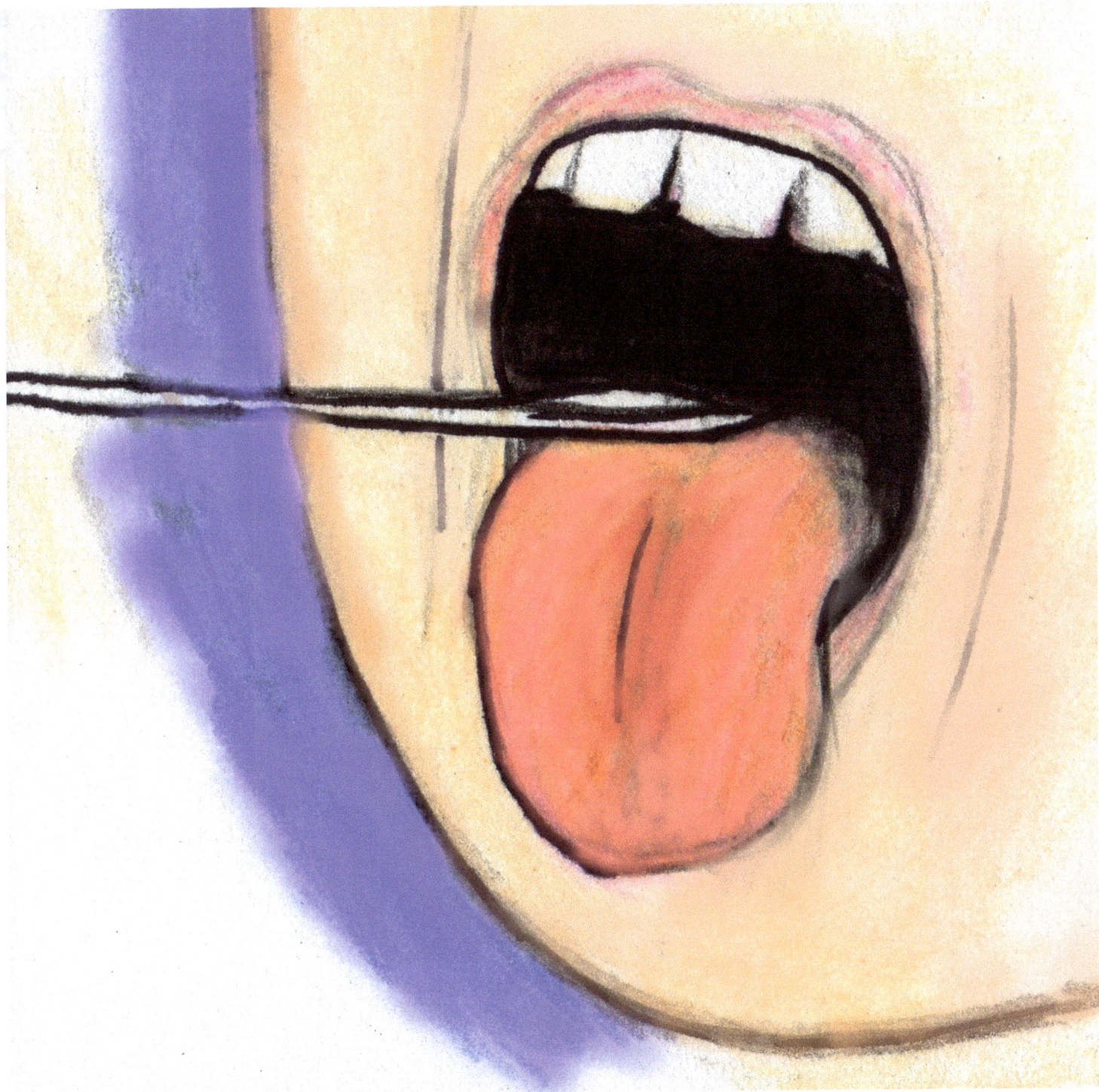

Dr. Michele explained to Mommy and Daddy that she would remove adenoids way in the back of my throat.
That's another big word.
Let's spell and sound it out.

A-D-E-N-O-I-D-S

Very good!

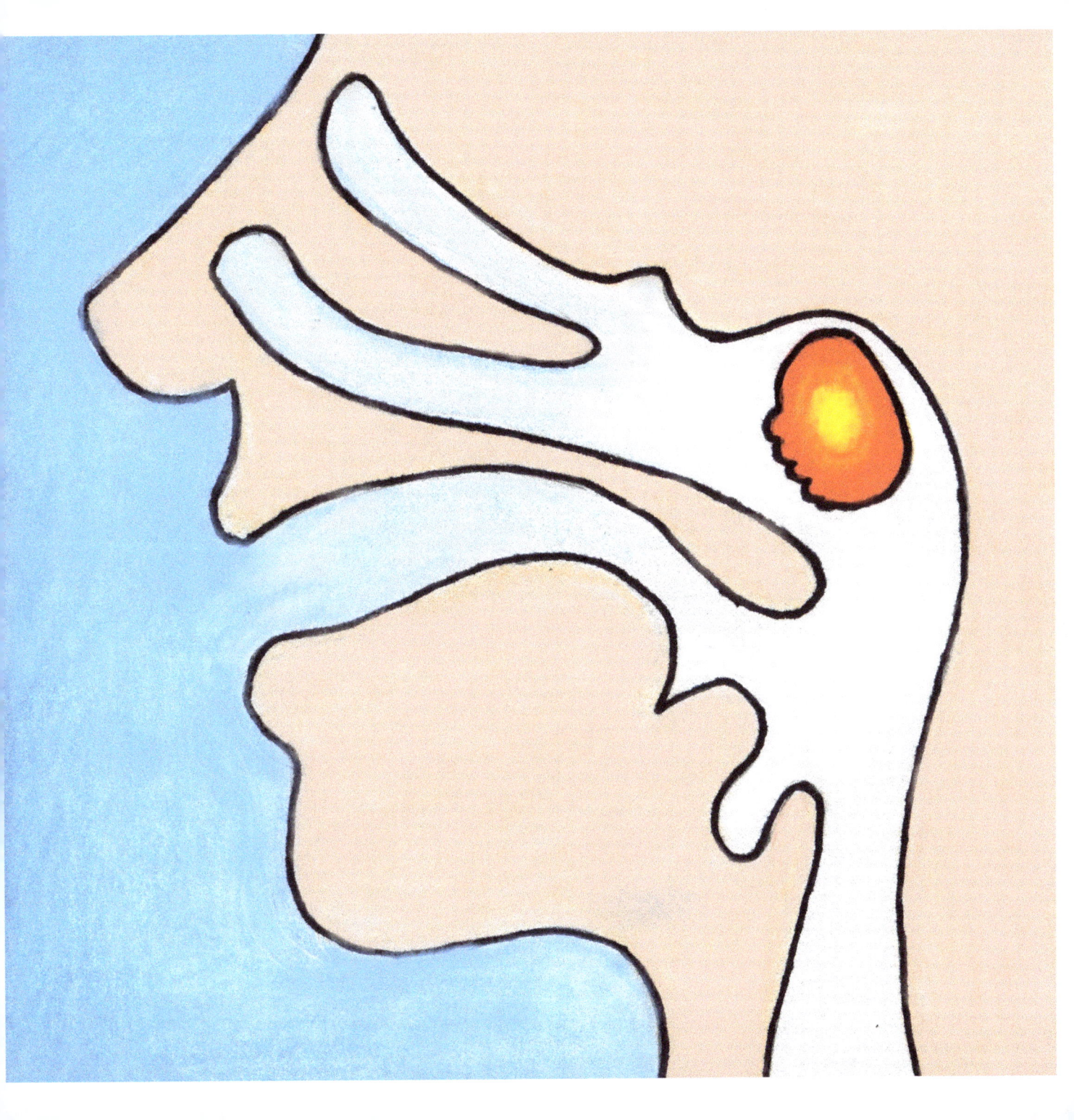

Dr. Michele would also place tubes in my ears.
What she was going to do would help me
not get earaches or sore throats.
I was happy about that,
but it also scared me.

Dr. Michele saw that I was scared.

"Carmelo," she said, "you will wear a mask
like Super-Heroes wear and
you will have to take deep breaths.
You will go to sleep and dream of having fun.
When you wake up, you can go home."

"I like fun and I like Super-Heroes,"
I said to Dr. Michele, but I was still scared.

"My favorite is SUPERMAN!"
Who is your favorite Super-Hero?

Mommy and Daddy told me all about my surgery.
"Carmelo, it's okay to be scared, but we will be there with you.
When we go home, you can have ice cream."

I do love ice cream, I thought.
My favorite is strawberry. What is yours?

When we got to the hospital,
the nurses met me, Mommy and Daddy.
I was already wearing my favorite pajamas.
They had lots of Super-Heroes on them.

The nurse put a big silly gown on me.
I got in a big bed with wheels.

"This is going to be fun, a bed with wheels.
Push me fast!" I said excitedly.
Mommy and Daddy gave me kisses and hugs.
"We'll be right here waiting for you," they said.
Okay, Carmelo. Hold on, here we go," said the nurse.
Off we went to the room where Dr. Michele was waiting.

"Hi, Carmelo. Remember, I told you about
the mask you will wear like the Super-Heroes?
It's right here. But before I put it on you,
we are going to have fun now," Dr. Michele said.

I heard music, and everyone in the room started dancing.
I sat up and started to dance too.
I showed Dr. Michele and the nurses how I could
dance with my dance moves. It WAS fun.

Do you like to dance?
Do you have a special dance you like to do?

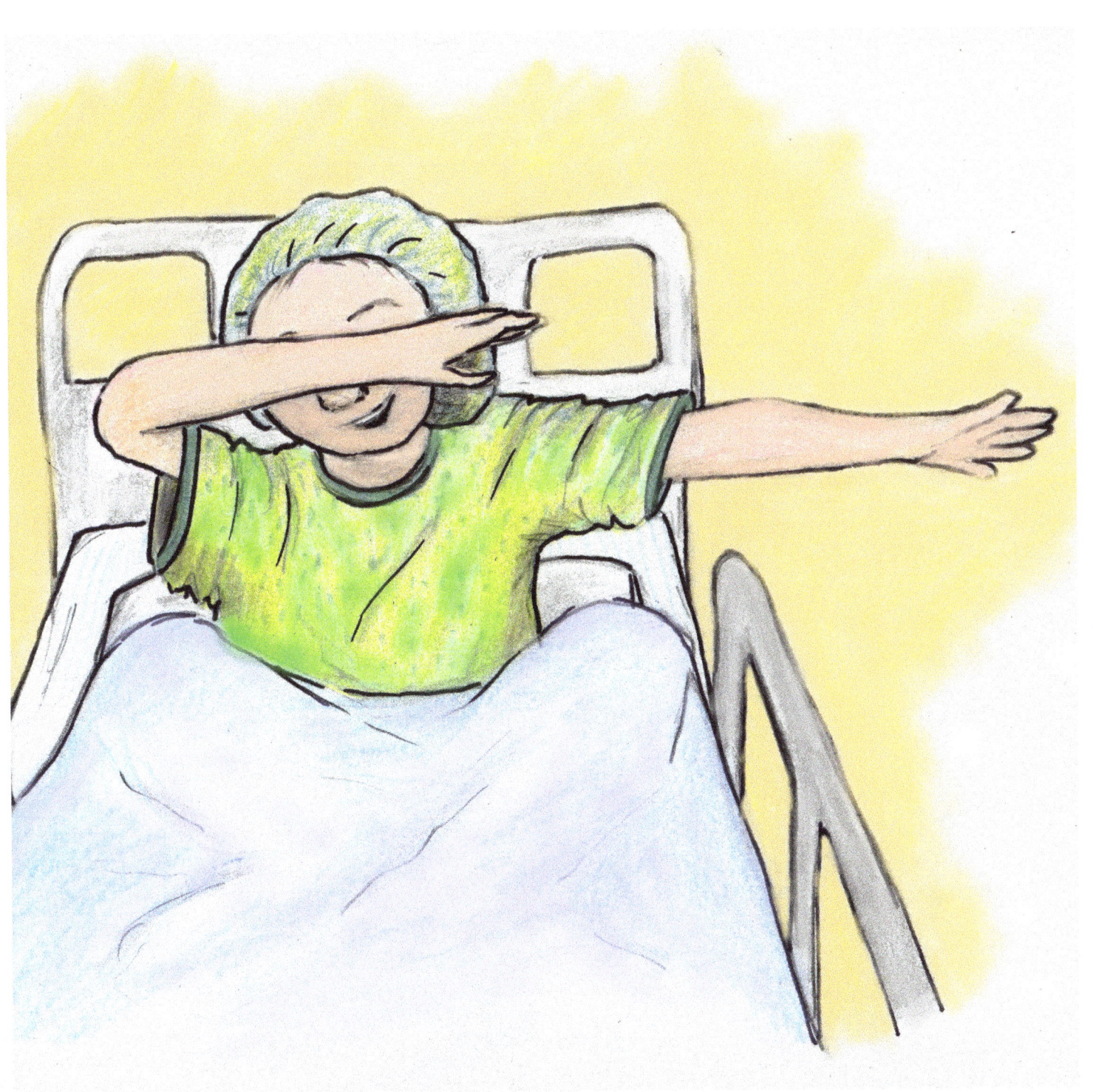

"Okay, Carmelo.
I'm going to put the mask on you now.
It's going to smell like grapes," Dr. Michele said.
"I like grapes," I said.

"Take deep breaths," they said.
Soon, I was asleep.

When I woke up, Mommy and Daddy were waiting for me.

Daddy said, "Carmelo,
Dr. Michele told us that you
listened and followed instructions
and you truly are a Super-Hero.

We know it scared you, but you were brave!"
"We are so proud of you," Mommy said.
"Let's go home and you can have some ice cream."

The End!

This is Carmelo on his way
to his doctor's appointment
with his favorite rag doll Monkey.

Thank you for reading another story of Carmelo's Adventures. This is an important part of my journey as an author... having readers. One way to enrich readership and have others enjoy my stories is through reviews. Please help by posting a review at either Amazon, Barnes & Noble, Books-A-Million ,I-books, Kindle, or Nook.

Look for other "Adventures of Carmelo™

About the Author

Mr. Berri graduated Columbia State University with an online business degree. He moved his family to Florida, from New York, spending years as a Financial Specialist with one of the largest banking institutions in the U.S. He has volunteered teaching Junior Achievement in the Florida public school district. In addition, he led a volunteer group for a reading program from grades K-3. During his career, he has done public speaking and appeared in a few TV commercials including voice overs. Berri has written many murder mysteries and children's books located on his website: fredberri.com

www.ingramcontent.com/pod-product-compliance
Lightning Source LLC
Chambersburg PA
CBHW040245100426
42811CB00011B/1158